Destination
COFFEE

Jane Ormond
Illustrations by Wenjia Tang

Hardie Grant

TRAVEL

Contents

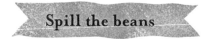
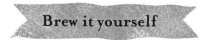

The world in a cup

COFFEE DESTINATIONS

Introduction

Ah, coffee. What makes this bean so magical? This crazy brown pill that we crush up to drink down, then skip off with a spring in our step? In a nutshell, coffee is our confidence in a cup.

·

It's there when you land in a new city, deciding which cafe is going to be 'your' cafe. Sitting on a breezy stoop, reading in a cafe, padding back to bed on a Sunday morning – it's all just better with coffee. Coffee wraps its mystical aroma around you and makes everything just a bit – more.

But coffee's not *just* coffee anymore. The humble cup has gone next level. The third-wave has elevated the global coffee scene to champion pour-overs and cold brews made with sustainable, single-origin beans. We see roasters working directly with coffee farmers and we taste the delicious outcomes in cafes all over the world.

You can sip thick Turkish coffee in the bazaars of Istanbul, or tour the coffee plantations of Vietnam. You can find specialty coffee in the laneways of Melbourne, or in the warehouse districts of downtown Honolulu. From a hard shot of espresso in an ornate, historic cafe in Venice to a clay pot of café de olla in a lo-fi cafe in Mexico City, coffee is a staple, a comfort, and an experience wherever we go in the world.

So let's go get coffee. Let's find the best cold brew. Let's practise our latte art. Let's find the most obscure brews in the most far-flung places, or let's try to make them for ourselves.

I need another cup. *Let's go!*

Spill
the beans

THE ORIGINS OF COFFEE

Birth of the bean

Dear coffee lover,

Meet the coffee plant, covered in coffee cherries. Inside those cherries is where you'll find actual coffee beans.

The cherries are picked and processed and the beans are extracted and dried.

The beans are then exported to coffee buyers for roasting and selling to you.

Now get your barista to recommend some interesting beans to try.

You'll be in for a delicious ride!

The discovery of coffee

Coffee originated in the 15th century in Ethiopia,
but the precise details of its discovery are shrouded
in kooky legend. The most popular story is that a
goat herder called Kaldi noticed his goats getting
all hopped up after eating the red berries of a
tree — these turned out to be coffee cherries.
(Aw, goats with coffee jitters!)

·

Word of these magic berries and their zesty properties spread
east towards Yemen. By the 16th century, coffee was all the
rage in Persia, Egypt, Syria and Turkey, giving rise to coffee
houses known as 'Schools of the Wise' because people drank
coffee and shared their knowledge.

By the 17th century, coffee had hit Europe with similar gusto.
Coffee houses were springing up all over the continent.
Interestingly, Oxford's coffee houses were nicknamed 'Penny
Universities', as it cost just that to sit there, drink coffee
and learn a thing or two from your caffeinated compadres.
Around the same time, coffee also landed across the Atlantic
in New York.

Since demand was growing, so was the competition to grow coffee outside of Arabia. In the 17th century, the Dutch managed to cultivate coffee plants on the island of Java, then on nearby Sumatra. In 1723, French naval officer Gabriel de Clieu sailed to Martinique, nursing coffee seedlings he got from the Jardin des Plantes in Paris, and the plants went gangbusters, kicking off future plantations in the Caribbean, South America and Central America.

But the best story is how coffee (supposedly) landed in Brazil at around the same time. Lieutenant Colonel Francisco de Mello Palheta was sent from Brazil to French Guiana to get coffee seedlings, but the French didn't want to share. So Francisco put the moves on the French governor's wife. They obviously worked because she gave him a bouquet of flowers when he left – with coffee shoots stashed inside. Hey presto – Brazil is now the world's biggest coffee-producing country. All from one bouquet and a couple of stolen glances.

Battle of the beans

When cafes promote a seasonal house blend, it's a reminder that coffee is actually a seasonal fruit, with characteristics that can vary from year to year.

Coffee generally grows in the 'coffee belt' – roughly that nice, warm section of the planet that sits between the Tropic of Cancer and the Tropic of Capricorn. We're talking parts of Africa, Central America, South America, the Middle East and Asia, as well as Hawaii, Puerto Rico and Jamaica.

Arabica and robusta are the two main strains of the coffee plant. Brazil is the largest producer of arabica beans, while Vietnam produces the most robusta.

Arabica plants grow at a higher altitude than robusta and the beans have less caffeine and more sugar, making for a sweet, bright brew. They're a little harder to grow and you don't get as many beans, so arabica beans are a bit more expensive.

Robusta plants thrive at a lower altitude. They're easier to grow than arabica and yield a lot more fruit, but the beans are smaller and have much more caffeine (caffeine acts like a natural pesticide) and much less sugar. This results in a cheaper, but more bitter, bean. Robusta beans are generally used for products like instant coffee.

Just as specific grapes result in different wines, different coffee varieties result in a different cup. Many beans are hybrids or mutations of the two main species, and will vary in terms of yield, flavour and ease of growth. For instance, some varieties are bred for abundant, low-hanging growth, making them easy to pick.

From the arabica plant, common varieties include the original typica, bourbon (a mutation of typica), caturra (a mutation of bourbon) and so on. Mundo Novo is an example of a hybrid – a cross between a typica and bourbon plant. The characteristics of the varieties are highlighted in the roasting.

So what's the deal with single-origins? It means the beans are sourced exclusively from one region or farm, meaning you're getting a very specific taste of an area.

A good roasting

Once coffee beans have been processed at their point of origin and are ready for export, they're called 'green beans' — that just means they haven't been roasted yet. Green beans stay stable for 12–18 months. Once they're roasted, they taste good for about a month, then they start to lose some flavour.

.

Here's how roasting happens: green beans are poured into a large, preheated drum and agitated while being heated. The temperature is increased incrementally to around 210°C (410°F) and when the beans are roasted to the level required, they're ejected into a cooling tray, swiftly brought down to room temperature and packed.

How long you roast beans for will affect the flavour. The shorter the time, the lighter the roast (as favoured in Oslo, *see* p. 72, or Copenhagen, *see* p. 73). The longer the time, the darker the roast (as favoured in Italian espresso, *see* p. 74). Around 10 minutes should give you a medium 'city' roast. A master roaster will know just how long to roast specialty beans to really tease out the flavour notes they want to highlight.

PROCESSING COFFEE BEANS

Processing refers to how the coffee bean is actually removed from the coffee cherry. How they're processed affects their flavour.

Natural (full bodied)
Cherries are laid out in the sun to dry, then hulled to separate the beans from the dried exterior.

Pulped natural (halfway between natural and washed)
The cherry skin is mechanically removed, then the stripped beans are dried in the sun. They have a honey sweetness.

Washed (clean and tea-like)
A mechanical 'depulper' removes the fruit flesh, then the beans are soaked in water to ferment away any leftover flesh, then washed and dried.

Surfing the waves

Have you heard about the 'waves' of coffee
but you're not quite sure what they mean?
Here's the lowdown.

•

First-wave doesn't so much refer back to the genesis of coffee,
but more to the point when commercially produced coffee –
mainly instant – became readily available and was marketed
into the mainstream in the early 20th century.

Second-wave is when espresso coffee drinks and chain cafes
(think Starbucks) appeared on shopping streets in major global
cities and oversized, take-out coffee drinks became a 'lifestyle'
brand. We're talking roughly from the 1990s onwards.

Third-wave refers to an artisanal approach, with specialty
coffee roasters and baristas sourcing premium beans with
ethical provenance for a superior and considered coffee-
drinking experience.

Fourth-wave takes an even more scientific approach, designing
equipment based on a deep understanding of the properties
of coffee to make the perfect cup. You'll find cafes riding the
fourth-wave in cities like Berlin (*see* p. 70), Melbourne (*see*
p. 114), Tokyo (*see* p. 100) and San Francisco (*see* p. 40).

Brew it yourself

COFFEE AT HOME

How to taste coffee

Is coffee just harsh, dark and bitter? No!
When tasting coffee, just remember:
flavour + aroma = taste.

You might hear coffee being described as having notes
of ripe berries or shortbread or even tomato. Say what?
They're actually clever terms because they describe both
the notes and the sensations.

Professional tasters look for sweetness, mouth-feel, acidity, flavour and finish. Some common tasting categories are:

- green/vegetative/herbaceous
- sour/fermented
- fruity
- floral
- sweet
- nutty, chocolate
- spicy
- roasted.

Coffee described as having notes of chocolate or honey has a rich mouth-feel and aroma. Coffee described as floral tastes bright and light on your tongue. Once you get deep into it, you'll be able to taste geographic differences, processing differences and bean varieties – you'll be like a coffee detective.

If you want to challenge your coffee palate, many roasteries hold cupping sessions, where you do a comparative tasting of a selection of coffees.

How to make perfect coffee at home

'Coffee can be really simple. Just buy the best ingredients and put them together,' says Andy Gelman, co-founder of Melbourne's acclaimed Omar and the Marvellous Coffee Bird.

I don't know about you, but I think starting the day with a really good cup of coffee makes everything just so much better. It's the tastiest coping pill. But bad coffee? There is no bigger buzzkill. It can turn that frown even further down.

So we hit up Andy Gelman for his expert tips on how to banish bad beans and only make perfect coffee at home. This is what he said.

BUY THE BEST BEANS

No matter how hard you try, you can't squeeze a good cup of coffee out of sub-standard products, so develop a relationship with your local roastery and buy fresh-roasted, well-sourced beans with a flavour profile that matches how you're going to brew it. The beans should be fit for purpose – some are better for filter, others for espresso. One roast doesn't fit all. Buy the best milk you can, too (cafes will often sell you theirs).

GRIND THEM FRESH

Grinding beans is vital and the difference between pre-ground and freshly ground is huge. When you grind coffee and you smell that beautiful aroma, that's the flavour leaving. So you should grind fresh and brew straight away.

Hand grinders are easy, portable and super affordable, or you can get a decent conical electric grinder for a reasonable price. Even an average quality grinder is better than using pre-ground coffee. And avoid blade grinders as they heat up the grounds.

CHOOSE THE RIGHT EQUIPMENT

Basically, you just need a brewing device, a grinder, a good kettle and, most importantly, a water filter because, when you think of it, the majority of a cup of coffee is water. Brew your kettle to boiling point then let it sit for 30 seconds before pouring onto the grounds.

In terms of devices, eliminate the middle ground and either go super simple – a French press or a gold-mesh Ezicaf filter – or go top of the range with a professional machine. If you do decide to invest in an incredible machine, make sure you get trained properly, as they can be tricky. One happy medium is having a French press at home and going to an excellent cafe for a perfect espresso made on a prestige machine for a treat.

STORE IT RIGHT

Coffee tastes good for about a month after it's roasted, so make sure you go to a roaster who can give you that information. (You won't get that on bags of supermarket beans.) Store the beans somewhere dark and cool in a cupboard. Some people keep their coffee in the fridge or freezer, but taking beans from hot to cold and back again is bad for their shelf life – just keep them stable. If you need to keep them for longer than a month, chances are you're buying too much.

FIND YOUR SWEET SPOT

Sweetness is the holy grail. If you're tasting sweetness in your cup, then you're doing something right. If you want to finesse your flavour, try your brewing method with more coffee or less, brew it for longer or shorter, and find your signature flavour.

HOME BREWING

There's a number of options when it comes to making your coffee at home. Choose what suits your space, taste and budget, from advanced and electric, to as simple as can be. Be warned though – some coffee equipment is incredibly beautifully designed and can quickly lead to addiction!

AeroPress

Stovetop moka pot

Drip filter

Coffee-for-one filter

Espresso machine

French press

Pour-over
(Chemex & V60)

What'll it be?

A COFFEE MENU GUIDE

Americano/long black – espresso and hot water. Start your Berlin (*see* p. 70) coffee odyssey with one.

Cafe mocha – espresso, chocolate, hot milk and foam. Turin's (*see* p. 22) signature version is addictive.

Cappuccino – equal parts espresso, steamed milk and foam. Warm up with one in London (*see* p. 62).

Drip filter – hot water filtered through ground coffee. Try a single-origin one in Portland (*see* p. 38).

Espresso – a strong shot of pressure-brewed black coffee. Perfected at iconic Pellegrini's in Melbourne (*see* p. 114).

Flat white – similar to a cappuccino but with more milk and a thin layer of microfoam. Order one in Auckland (*see* p. 119), say you thought it was an Australian invention and sit back.

Latte – similar to a cappuccino but milkier, and with less foam. Have it with your Parisian (*see* p. 66) breakfast.

Macchiato – small format, espresso shot with a dab of foam. A great way to taste Cape Town's (*see* p. 96) local roasts.

Piccolo – small format, equal parts espresso and milk. Quick and ideal in New York (*see* p. 46).

Pour-over – hot water gently poured over coffee grounds by hand into a conical filter, such as V60. Make it your San Francisco (*see* p. 40) choice as you research your favourite roasters.

Ristretto – short-pulled espresso. Order one standing at a classic bar in Rome (*see* p. 76).

Nitro cold brew
Looks like Guinness, tastes like coffee. Head to Austin's (*see* p. 42) Cuvée Coffee for a whole coffee brewery's worth.

Cold brew
Made from grounds steeped in cold water over hours. Have a refresher after surfing in Byron Bay (*see* p. 117).

KEEPING IT COOL
What do you do when it's just too damn hot for coffee? Try these:

Cascara soda
Made from the dried flesh of the coffee cherry. Perfect for beating São Paulo's (*see* p. 52) heat.

Espresso tonic
Tonic water over ice with a shot of espresso and an orange wedge. A jazzy New Orleans (*see* p. 44) cooldown drink.

Global coffee at home

Want to go on a global coffee adventure from the comfort of your own kitchen? Try these easy brews from around the world.

.

TURKISH COFFEE ISTANBUL-STYLE

For this recipe you will need a cezve (a small tapered cooking pot with a long handle, but you can use a small saucepan if you don't have one). Cezves are readily available from coffee equipment stores, kitchenware stores and online.

Pour 1 cup of water and 1 tsp of white sugar into the cezve or saucepan and bring to the boil.

Remove from the heat and stir in 1 tbsp of powder-fine coffee (you can add a crushed cardamom pod or ⅛ tsp of ground cardamom here for added flavour) and bring it to the boil until it foams.

Remove from the heat again and let the boiling foam drop, then return it to let it boil and foam up again.

Remove from the heat one last time, let it settle for a moment then carefully pour into small cups and serve with Turkish delight.

VIETNAMESE COFFEE HANOI-STYLE

For a take on the cà phê sữa đá recipe you will need a phin (a cup-sized stainless steel filter, available from most Asian grocers).

Spoon 1–3 tbsp of condensed milk into a glass (depending on how sweet you like it).

Pack 3 tbsp of dark roasted coffee grounds (Vietnamese coffee if you can get it) into the phin and sit it on top.

Add boiling water and let the brew slowly drip through the phin and into the sweet milk.

Stir the milk through the coffee and drink – filter it over ice if you want a cool version for warm days.

Don't have a phin? Sub in a shot of strong black coffee instead.

MEXICAN COFFEE MEXICO CITY–STYLE

Café de olla is traditionally prepared in a clay pot, but it can be adapted and works on the stovetop. In a saucepan, place:

· 2 cinnamon sticks
· 2 cloves
· ¼ cup of brown sugar
· rind of 1 orange
· 6 cups of water

Bring to the boil, then reduce the heat and cook until the sugar has dissolved. Keeping it on a reduced heat, add 6 tbsp of ground coffee and stir, leaving it to simmer and infuse for a few minutes, then strain it over cups to serve. (Optional spicy additions include Mexican chocolate or cocoa powder, vanilla or a pinch of cayenne pepper.)

CAFÉ CUBANO HAVANA-STYLE

Make a pot of stovetop coffee. As it's beginning to brew, remove a tablespoon or two of it and drop into a jug (pitcher) with ⅓ cup of white sugar and return the pot to the stove. Whisk the sugar and coffee until pale and foamy.

Stir in the rest of the coffee from the stovetop, let the foam float to the top, and serve immediately.

Make it a cafe con leche (coffee with hot milk) by pouring it into warmed milk. Just make sure that 'espuma' is on top. It's all about the foam.

BICERIN TURIN-STYLE

This signature drink from Turin is the ultimate mocha.

Pour ½ cup of espresso over ⅓ cup of chopped dark chocolate and stir until it melts.

Put 2 tsp of sugar and 1 tsp of cocoa powder in a saucepan with a dash of the coffee/chocolate mix and stir to a smooth paste. Then add the rest of the liquid and stir over a low heat until completely smooth.

Pour into small wine glasses and gently top with barely whipped cream.

GREEK FRAPPÉ ATHENS-STYLE

Put 2 tsp of instant coffee, 2 tsp of white sugar and 2 tbsp of cold water into a jar with a tight-fitting lid and shake, shake, shake it until it's foamy.

Take a glass half-filled with ice cubes, pour the foamy coffee over them and top it off with cold water.

If you want a creamy taste, add cream, condensed milk or evaporated milk.

COFFEE BODY SCRUB

So you're relaxing with your Sunday morning coffee and you feel like a little pampering. Don't throw your grounds out! Here's a quick body scrub recipe for that caffeinated day spa vibe.

Grab a small bowl and add:

- 3 tbsp of ground coffee
- 2 tbsp of olive oil
- 1 tbsp of brown sugar
- 2–3 drops of vanilla extract

Stir it all together into a chunky paste then hop in the shower, massage it onto your skin then rinse it off. You'll feel silky and smell delicious.
(Don't keep any leftovers.)

Latte art

Want to pep up your latte art? Here are ways to add a bit of flair to your foam.

·

STENCIL IT!
Add some street art to your coffee with a set of chocolate powder stencils, so you can adorn foamed milk with any number of cute designs.

TRY FUDGE ART
Get a squeezy bottle with a fine nozzle and fill it with chocolate syrup to decorate the foam with a range of high-contrast, chocolatey designs.

Start by doing a spiral, then use a toothpick to drag lines out from the centre to create a starburst. Drag the line inwards instead and you've got a flower. Drop little blobs in a row and pull the toothpick down through the middle of each blob and you've created a chain of hearts.

FREE-POUR ART

This is where you free-pour a cafe-style heart or a rosetta onto the surface of your latte. (You need a steady hand for latte art, so ease off on the espressos beforehand!)

Follow these steps to get started ...

Prepare your espresso.

Now steam your milk (whole milk works best). It should be the texture of wet paint.

Swirl the espresso around the cup, tilt the cup and start pouring an even stream of milk from a jug (pitcher) into the centre of the cup, keeping your jug a couple of inches away from the cup. Mix the coffee and milk together so you get an even brown surface to work your design onto.

When the cup is about three-quarters full, the foam will start to rise to the top. Bring your jug right down close to the cup, tip it slightly to speed up the pour, and very gently wiggle it to create a tight, white zig-zag of foam. Imagine you're gently sketching with a pencil. Draw the spout back up, untilt the cup, then dash it up through the middle of the pattern to create a heart. To make a rosetta, make a more elongated zig-zag.

Remember to pour high and slow, then low and fast.

ADD DETAILS

Once you've mastered free pouring, you can start adding details to your designs by etching – using the darker background foam to add details.

Let's say you're making a heart with a smiley face. Free pour the heart then get a toothpick, dip it into the darker parts of the surface and dot it into the white parts for the eyes and the mouth.

To create starbursts or trailing designs, dip a clean toothpick into the white sections and flick it outwards.

TIPS FROM THE BEST

Take your latte art to the next level with these tips from Shinsaku Fukayama, Australian Barista Champion, World Latte Art finalist and designer of the Katana milk jug (specifically designed for accurate and precise latte art):

· Master the basics first. Make that perfect heart before tackling more detailed designs.

· Keep an eye on cup size. Take into account how much espresso is in the cup and how much milk you'll need. Too much milk in the jug makes it too hard to control. Your milk should run out just as you're finishing off your design.

· Practise, practise, practise. If you don't want to waste gallons of milk and coffee practising, there are plenty of hacks to try, including steaming up dish soap in water. It foams up just like milk! (Shinsaku practised using water and pepper.)

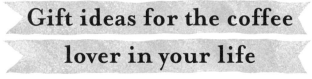

Gift ideas for the coffee lover in your life

(WHICH MIGHT BE YOU)

If you're a coffee lover, or you have one in your life, you know that it's a love that knows no bounds. Which makes them (or you) super easy to shop for when it comes to gift-giving time.

·

Here are some suggestions:

· a coffee subscription – customised beans from a favourite roaster, delivered regularly

· an air-tight coffee vault in a snappy colour

· a travel bag specifically for your AeroPress

· a super glamorous ceramic coffee brewer

· a collapsible pour-over for travel

· a sigh-worthy Takahiro kettle

· a be-your-own-barista course – a lot of major roasters offer training, and some offer online courses in the more scientific or business-related side of coffee, too.

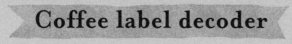

WHAT'S IN MY BAG?

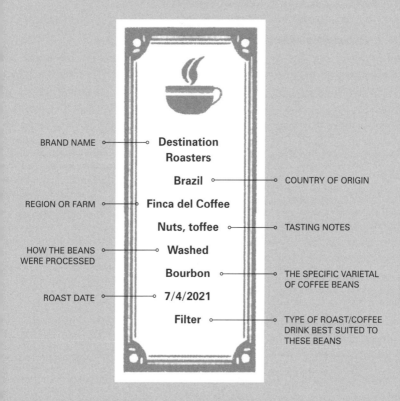

BRAND NAME — Destination Roasters

Brazil — COUNTRY OF ORIGIN

REGION OR FARM — Finca del Coffee

Nuts, toffee — TASTING NOTES

HOW THE BEANS WERE PROCESSED — Washed

Bourbon — THE SPECIFIC VARIETAL OF COFFEE BEANS

ROAST DATE — 7/4/2021

Filter — TYPE OF ROAST/COFFEE DRINK BEST SUITED TO THESE BEANS

The world in a cup

COFFEE DESTINATIONS

North America

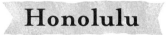

Honolulu

Just the thought of Hawaii makes you bliss out.
The beaches, the madly blue water, the swaying palms
and the handsome volcanos. Hawaii also happens to
be an island paradise for coffee lovers.

·

Hawaii grows a lot of very well-regarded coffee, thanks to that crisp volcanic water and rich soil. Kona on the Big Island is Hawaii's biggest, most famed growing region (Waialua on O'ahu is Honolulu's closest growing region). The wondrous thing about Hawaiian coffee is how it varies from island to island. You can really taste the terrain. Hawaii's coffee farming is a multi-generational affair, so the locals know the land intimately, and know what to expect from it. Many Honolulu roasters have close relationships with the farmers, and as a traveller you can visit some of the coffee farms, too.

Kona coffee is grown in the small Kona Coffee Belt on the Big Island. A combination of morning sun, afternoon clouds and showers, with rich, well-drained volcanic soil and perfect tropical temperatures make for superb beans with a very clean finish. If you want to buy some, make sure it's authentic 100 per cent Kona, as the 'Kona blends' often have very little Kona in them.

> The wondrous thing about Hawaiian coffee is how it varies from island to island.

You'll find some sensational cafes in Honolulu, from the vaulted, spacious Kona Coffee Purveyors with its b. Patisserie to the breezy white, plant-strewn Arvo with its bright umbrellas outside. There's the art-filled, vintage feel of Ars Cafe and some deceptively simple cafes like Morning Glass with its beach shack vibe and killer guest roasts.

Look out for roasters like Big Island Roasters and Rusty's Hawaiian or head to the Kapi'olani Community College Farmer's Market on a Saturday morning to try the Maui coffee from Koko Crater Coffee Roasters – it's dynamic. If you can lever yourself off the sand at Waikiki, go exploring downtown Honolulu and Chinatown where you'll find some interesting bars, stores, old-school bakeries and local produce markets.

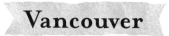

Vancouver

The seeds of Vancouver's coffee scene were planted by
European migrants in the 1940s and '50s; Vancouver
was the first international outpost of Starbucks,
opening in 1987; and the city's current coffee scene
is one of internationally awarded roasters, baristas
and latte artists. It's little wonder that Vancouver can
deliver a stellar cup of ethically sourced joe.

•

With its brisk weather and picturesque surrounding mountains
and waterways, Vancouver's one of those great cities to
actually drink coffee in too.

Vancouver also has a luscious food scene – a tasty stroll
through the bustling Granville Island Public Market showcases
a snapshot of the city's diverse local produce, artisan bakers
and signature dishes to cosy up with at a communal table.

Latte artist and master roaster Brian Turko of Milano Coffee
has won multiple gold medals internationally for his espresso
blends, and you'll find branches of Milano all across the city.
Similarly, head to Prado for coffee made by Sammy Piccolo,
a Canadian Barista Champion and the first ever winner of the
World Latte Art Championships.

You'll find stunning cafes all over Vancouver – explore areas like Commercial Drive in the city's north-east, which is full of great cafes and delis. The warehouse district of Yaletown is a striking area, home to coffee notables like Caffe Artigiano, JJ Bean Coffee Roasters and Matchstick. Pretty Kitsilano is a scenic patch where you'll find the famed, sustainably sourced beans of 49th Parallel Coffee Roasters and Lucky's Doughnuts, or head to the slightly grungy but gently gentrifying Gastown and settle yourself in at Timbertrain or Revolver, which features a rotating brew menu from their favourite boutique roasters.

A CANADIAN INSTITUTION
Sure, you're all third-wave, but you've got to try a double-double at Tim Hortons just once – black coffee with two creams and two sugars.

West Coast USA

A SERIOUSLY SERIOUS COFFEE SCENE

With the world-famous java jewels of the Pacific
Northwest and high-tech brews of San Francisco,
this patch of the USA is coffee paradise.

So you love coffee? Um, why aren't you living in Portland
already?! Bisected by the Willamette River and surrounded
by lush and mountainous landscapes, Portland has a villagey
vibe with its Craftsman houses, yoga studios and food truck
parks. It's known for its quirky mindset, artisanal food scene,
live music and ethically sourced, locally roasted and totally
perfect coffee.

Look out for local icons like Stumptown, Coava Coffee Roasters
(try a flight of their award-winning coffee), Albina Press, Water
Avenue and way too many more to list. Even seemingly divey
diners will proudly serve Portland Coffee Roasters coffee. And
in what might be the equivalent of caffeinated big bang, Proud
Mary (from fellow famous coffee city Melbourne, Australia) has
opened a branch in Portland.

Portland is fairly compact and walkable. Go exploring
neighbourhoods like Downtown and the area around NW 23rd
in the west, and Buckman, Mississippi and the Alberta Arts
District in the east to get this city's flavour.

Coffee is a way of life in Seattle, largely attributed to the cold, wet weather that makes hunkering indoors with a steaming pot of coffee so appealing, and Seattle has spawned more than its fair share of awarded baristas, ground-breaking coffee houses and innovative roasteries (and yes, Starbucks, that second-wave coffee juggernaut).

> You can ricochet from one caffeinated wonder to another.

Seattle is also a city that champions its local produce (just try a Bing cherry), so go exploring Pike Place Market for a snapshot of the Pacific Northwest's food scene and areas like Capitol Hill, Ballard and Belltown for thoughtfully crafted Seattle-style coffee.

While it's impossible to pick out cafe highlights in this divinely caffeinated city, it's worth putting Café Allegro, Seattle's oldest espresso bar, on your list.

The pioneering spirit is writ large over San Francisco, from its gold rush to its countercultural boom and then its high-tech explosion. The Golden City's coffee history can be traced hand in hand with these changes – from the establishment of Folgers in the 1850s, on to the Italian cafes and the beatnik enclaves like Vesuvio in the 1950s, then the rise of the local roasters like Sightglass,

Wrecking Ball, Boot, Blue Bottle, Ritual, Four Barrel, Equator, Andytown, Verve … the list is as epic as its quality is high.

Here, baristas take an artful, scientific approach to their coffee and, like zig-zagging down Lombard Street, you can ricochet from one caffeinated wonder to another, whether that's a simple diner coffee in the Castro or a Blue Bottle amidst the gourmet treats of the iconic Ferry Building.

THE LUCK OF THE IRISH
It's a bit kitsch and a lot touristy, but everyone should try an Irish Coffee at San Francisco's Buena Vista at least once. It's been serving this whisky-laced, cream-topped coffee since the early 1950s and it's hypnotic to watch the high-speed bartenders whipping up a whole row of them.

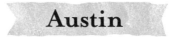

Austin

COLD BREWS AND GOOD TIMES

If you want a dose of Texan hospitality with a hearty dash of quirk and a massive side of artisanal produce, Austin has it in spades. This charming, artful, laidback city, famous for attracting music, film and media fans to its annual South by Southwest festival, has an effervescent food scene and a coffee scene to match.

•

Specialty coffee kicked off in Austin in the early 2000s and now a sensational single-origin or a considered pour-over showcasing superior beans is a given. Austin was also an early proponent of cold brew coffee and canned nitro cold brew – a keep-it-cool necessity to beat the Texas heat.

Go strolling Downtown and you'll discover a clutch of great cafes, including the much-lauded Houndstooth ('The pattern of coffee and people'), the spaciously minimal, two-storey Medici, and the relaxed and airy Merit. Further over east, you'll find Fleet and its innovative 'Coffee and …' offerings, like the Flip-Top which combines espresso with root beer spices, chicory root and nitro.

You'll also find bright white Figure 8 Coffee Purveyors and its excellent personalised mugs, and the super-cute Flitch that serves coffee and pastries out of an old campervan. Austin's famous Cuvée Coffee and its spacious coffee bar also has a cold coffee brewery, where they serve nitro cold brew with added extras like hemp oil or horchata (*see* p. 19). (Are you googling Austin rentals yet?) Around the city, you'll see signs that say 'Keep Austin Weird'. Weird? Keep it caffeinated!

New Orleans

HISTORY AND DIVERSITY IN A CUP

Steamy, jazzy, delicious — New Orleans is a cultural hedonist's goldmine. With the unbridled madness of Mardi Gras, the joy of the New Orleans Jazz and Heritage Festival and the swampy grooves of various blues and roots festivals, it's simultaneously historic and contemporary. The sizzle of innovative Creole restaurants scents the air, music swims through the sticky breeze, and ornate French Quarter townhouses frame the scene for all the good times that are about to roll.

.

Let's take a tasty little history lesson, because coffee runs deep in New Orleans's veins. Green coffee was initially imported from the Caribbean in the late 1700s but, when the Civil War broke out and supplies were harder to come by, coffee lovers got creative by supplementing it with locally grown and roasted chicory, which tastes similar to coffee. This distinctive blend is still popular as a classic New Orleans brew.

Then, in the early 1800s, Rose Nicaud, a former slave who had purchased her freedom, set up a portable cart in New Orleans's famous French Market. She's credited as being the city's first street vendor to sell freshly brewed coffee. She offered it straight up or with warmed milk (café au lait) and she inspired other businesses that then shaped the city's identity of coffee, like Café Du Monde – a local chain established at the French Market in 1862 and known for its coffee and beignets (like a powdered sugar doughnut).

Today the city boasts small cafes happily pouring nostalgic brews of café au lait with chicory, as well as indie cafes and incredible small-batch roasters like Mammoth Espresso that showcase prime beans.

For first-timers, dive into the multitude of classic cafes in the French Quarter, then head beyond the tourist areas to the Warehouse District to discover the indie scene. Handy hint: an espresso tonic (*see* p. 19) is the perfect coffee hit when you need to beat The Big Easy's heat.

New York City

New York City is synonymous with coffee — a high-speed city fuelled by a ravenous intake of caffeine anywhere, anytime. From Italian espresso bars to all-American diners, from beatnik coffee houses to contemporary warehouse roasters, it's no wonder New York is called the city that never sleeps. It's been hopped up on caffeine the whole time!

·

Coffee has been the lifeblood and cultural wingman of this magical city. By 1790, New York had become the most populous city in the USA, and by 1793 it was roasting up a storm. In the 1920s, Domenico Parisi introduced the city to the magic of the cappuccino at his Caffe Reggio in Greenwich Village, an area that would go on to be known for its beatnik and bohemian coffee houses that attracted renegade writers, poets, artists and musicians. Take a book and head for this New York institution. Don't forget to tip your hat to Domenico's original espresso machine, possibly the oldest in the city – made in 1902.

Brooklyn's and Manhattan's coffee scenes have boomed.

Brooklyn's and Manhattan's coffee scenes have boomed, from diner filters to homegrown roasts, boutique roasteries and stylish drip bars. Waverly Diner is a 24/7 favourite still slinging coffee and eggs at all hours. The iconic, bright orange Mud coffee truck that started in 2001 has now retired its wheels, but you can still get your Mud at the Mudpark kiosk on the Lower East Side or at its all-day diner, Mudspot, in the East Village. A psychedelic bag of its coffee beans makes a great take-home gift.

The new millennium saw an influx of Australian-style coffee slingers like Ruby's, Little Collins and Bluestone Lane keen to bring flat whites and avocado toast to the Big Apple. In this city, you'll be sure to find your moment.

Mexico City

A fiesta of colour and flavour, Mexico City is a vibrant, teeming metropolis, brimming with energy against a backdrop of scenic, colonial-era buildings. An effervescent clash of tradition and contemporary culture, it delivers street art and an innovative food scene alongside historic sites and classic cantinas.

·

The traditional Mexican coffee is café de olla – coffee, cinnamon and raw cane sugar prepared in a clay pot. It's rich and spiced and lovely on a cold day (*see* recipe p. 21). With Mexico City having so much incredible coffee within reach, there are some inventive (and chic) coffee houses really pushing this local product into the spotlight and keenly promoting the farm-to-cup concept.

You can get every brewing option here, from V60 to AeroPress and anything beyond, but the beauty of seeking out the coffee innovators is the way they capture the true flavour of Mexican coffee. Drip owns its own coffee farm; Almanegra showcases Mexican microlots; and Café Buna works directly with Mexican farmers. Café Avellaneda roasts its Mexican coffee in-house and the owner is a past Mexican Brewers Cup Champion. Neighbourhoods like Condesa and Roma will reward you with some thrilling caffeinated discoveries.

WITHIN BREWING DISTANCE
Mexico City also has renowned coffee growing regions. Areas like Coatepec, Veracruz, Oaxaca and Chiapas produce beautiful beans. They vary within regions but you can expect beans that are light-bodied and low in acidity, some with notes of nuts and chocolate.

South America
& the Caribbean

SÃO PAULO

HAVANA

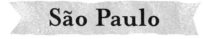

São Paulo

BRAZILIAN BREWS

Brazil is the world's biggest coffee producer so you've got to make a pilgrimage and get a cup straight from the source, right? For a caffeinated urban adventure, head to pulsing São Paulo, where you can get lost in this enormous city thronging with street art and incredible restaurants and teeming with millions of people — but where you can also take a private tour of nearby coffee plantations to get up close to the beloved bean.

·

The traditional coffee here is cafezinho – sugar and water is heated in a pan, coffee grounds are stirred in, then it's removed from the heat and poured through a filter. Scalded milk is an optional addition. Team this sweet brew with a pão de queijo (Brazilian cheese bread) at a corner bakery for a cosy start to the day. Then it's time to explore São Paulo's third-wave cafes, many of which work closely with particular Brazilian farmers.

If your coffee geekery knows no bounds, make a beeline for The Coffee Lab, an amazingly eco-conscious cafe, school and roastery focused on micro lots. It's run by internationally regarded barista Isabela Raposeiras, who sources particular beans from all over the country. You can have another farm-to-cup experience at Isso é Café – the owner harvests beans from his own farm. Sample these small batches with a V60 to really get the flavours.

Explore areas like Vila Madalena for hip stores, edgy galleries and the street art–filled Beco do Batman. Itaim Bibi is a super stylish patch, or head to Moema where you'll find a concentration of cafes as well as the sprawling Ibirapuera Park, if you need to take a breather from São Paulo's frenetic pace.

BRAZIL'S COFFEE REGIONS

Get to know some of Brazil's biggest coffee growing states (mainly in the south-east), including Minas Gerais (the biggest), Espírito Santo, São Paulo, Bahia, Rondônia and Paraná.

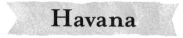

Havana

SWEET COFFEE AND CLASSIC CARS

Cuba's capital is a cinematic city with a constant
musical backbeat. Colourful colonial-era buildings
are adorned with archways, and streets are lined with
retro-glam cars from the 1950s, while the smell
of coffee wafts across Plaza Vieja from the patio
at Café El Escorial.

·

In Havana, coffee is intrinsically linked with socialising. Coffee
here is not so much about the beans in your cup – it's more
about the friends and family you share it with.

Stovetop moka pots are the most popular home-brewing
method here. A traditional café Cubano (sometimes called
cafecito) involves brewing a pot of coffee, taking a little of
it and whipping it with sugar so it looks light and frothy.
Some of the espuma (whipped brew) is spooned into a tacita
(miniature cup), then topped off with more black coffee
from the pot. The foamed coffee gives the look of the classic
espresso crema, and it's a small but mighty shot of strong,
sweet coffee (*see* recipe p. 22).

The other main Cuban coffee versions are cortadito (espresso topped with steamed milk – evaporated milk is also an option) or cafe con leche (coffee with hot milk – add a pinch of salt to heighten the flavour). Many people sell their own home-brewed coffee from their ventanillas (street-facing windows).

Cuba is home to three coffee growing regions (the Sierra Maestra mountains, Pinar del Río and Escambray) and Havana is home to some happening cafes and roasteries that showcase the local beans. Go exploring areas like Old Havana and Vedado, and try popular coffee houses like Café O'Reilly with its arched windows, colourful tiles and central spiral staircase, the warm-hued and cosy Café Arcangel, the technicolour Belview Art Café, or the almost Grecian vibe of the bright blue and white Café Bohemia that fronts onto the lively Plaza Vieja.

·

In Havana, coffee is intrinsically linked with socialising.

·

Europe

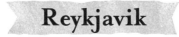

Reykjavik

THE LAND OF FIRE AND ICE(D) COFFEE

Compact, kooky and utterly charismatic, Reykjavik is small on population but huge on cultural appeal, sitting in that sweet spot between cosmopolitan and cosy. A buzzing, friendly cafe culture thrives amidst state-of-the-art museums, photogenic thermal pools, trail-blazing architecture and that wonderland that comes from almost 24 hours of sunlight in summer. Just beyond the city's doorstep, you'll find spectacular mountains, glaciers, volcanos and hot springs.

•

Iceland is one of the largest consumers of coffee in the world, and Reykjavik's cafe scene is rich, varied and full of personality. You won't find the major international chains here, but you will find a couple of small-scale local chains like Te & Kaffi, with its own roastery, and Kaffitár, whose staff manage close relationships with coffee farmers.

One of the city's biggest roasters is Reykjavik Roasters. A cafe, retailer and educator, it sources sustainable beans and works closely with the farms it imports from. Being a big rock in the middle of the North Atlantic doesn't make Iceland prime coffee farmland, but Reykjavik Roasters imports some very special seasonal beans that are well worth seeking out.

Go wandering Reykjavik's city centre and you'll happen upon all manner of quirky, unpretentious cafes, like Café Babalú with its bright orange exterior, an eclectic interior and free black coffee refills, while Iða Zimsen brings together books and brews. Mokka Kaffi is one of Reykjavik's oldest cafes – it started in 1958 and was the first one with an espresso machine serving Italian espresso. For the perfect example of Reykjavik cafe culture, settle into a soft velvet armchair at cosy Stofan Café, order a coffee, grab a friend and curl up over a board game.

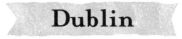

Dublin

Dublin's coffee scene might be small, but it's sure got some espresso kick. Rich in green spaces and literary history, this creative city, divided by the River Liffey, is home to a bunch of micro-roasters bucking the frappucino tsunami in favour of some seriously soulful coffee – and winning awards to boot.

·

You'll find glamour, cosiness and creative buzz within Dublin's cafe scene, from quirky, book-filled enclaves to architectural gleamers, and from coffee carts to cafes in film centres.

Karl Purdy was the instigator of Ireland's coffee scene, inspired by the coffee culture he soaked up during a few years in Canada. He opened The Ground Floor in Belfast in 1995, sold the super successful business just two years later, and moved to Dublin to open Coffeeangel, which started as a coffee cart in 2004 and is now a deeply ingrained part of Dublin's coffee fabric, with multiple outlets across the city.

Since then, a number of A-grade micro-roasters have set up shop. Look out for beans by Dublin roasters like Cloud Picker – you'll find its slender, stylish, bare-brick cafe next door to The Academy on Pearse Street (in what used to be The Academy's old projector room). You also shouldn't miss 3fe, started by an award-winning ex-Coffeeangel barista; Roasted Brown, which has its own cafe called Laine, My Love; and Urbanity, which sources its green beans from suppliers in coffee-mad Oslo (*see* p. 72).

Explore the pretty city centre, as well as pockets like Phibsboro, Stoneybatter and Portobello for a taste of Dublin's coffee culture.

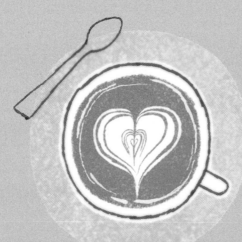

UK

Tea has traditionally been the drink of choice in the
UK, but now it's fuelled by coffee and you'll find
indie coffee scenes from London to Edinburgh.

•

London is a thrill ride of a city – a raucous, creative, multicultural
metropolis driven by history and fashion. Its coffee houses
of the 1700s were gathering spaces for intellectuals, and
the city's coffee lounge scene took flight in the late 1940s in
Soho, thanks to Italian immigrants. Fast forward to now and
it's riding the third-wave with ingenuity and passion. The
pioneering Monmouth Coffee has been roasting high-quality
beans since the late '70s. In 2008, Square Mile Coffee Roasters
began infiltrating cafes all over the city. Prufrock in Clerkenwell
is a coffee geek's idea of heaven. Aim your jitters at Soho,
Clerkenwell or Shoreditch, or check out coffee carts and stalls
at tasty markets, like Borough Market or Spitalfields.

Cardiff is Wales's laidback capital, a cultural charmer of a city,
with a medieval castle, historic arcades and the Cardiff Bay
waterfront. It boasts lush local roasts, heavy on an ethical
and sustainable approach. Hard Lines Café and Roastery is
one perfect, pocket-sized example in Cardiff Market, serving
cracking coffee – its large bottles of cold coffee are perfect

for a picnic in Bute Park. Burrow into the arcades and you'll stumble across Uncommon Ground Coffee Bar and Roastery, or award-winning The Plan. Grab a bag of single-origin from Lufkin in Pontcanna, or a nitro from Quantum Coffee Roasters in the arts and cultural centre.

Craft coffee thrives in creative Manchester. Magnificent mills from the city's manufacturing past have been transformed into vaulted cafes where there's no shortage of a Chemex. There's also a tight coffee roasting scene, with a clutch of Mancunian roasters, including Grindsmith, Passion Fruit, ManCoCo, Heart and Graft, Salford Roasters and Ancoats Coffee Co. TAKK offers a Scandi-centric vibe and a range of single-origins on the brew bar. Federal riffs on the classic Australian cafe. North Tea Power is a stalwart of the Manchester craft coffee scene, while Idle Hands is a must for coffee geeks. For a classic Italian espresso, try Lupo in Salford. Areas like Ancoats, the Northern Quarter and Chorlton are goldmines of innovative cafes.

For a cinematic place to cosy up with a coffee, Scotland's gaspingly gorgeous capital of Edinburgh is it. Edinburgh Castle creates a striking backdrop to the city's architecture – medieval in the Old Town, Georgian in the New Town, stunningly contemporary at the Parliament buildings. It's a sophisticated, student-y scene, full of snug basement cafes. Look out for excellent beans from Fortitude Coffee or Artisan Roast. Brew Lab showcases two different espressos and filters daily, roasted by Union Hand-Roasted Coffee, and offers coffee courses (in the basement, of course). For that secretive coffee experience, disappear into subterranean Wellington Coffee. Explore the areas of Broughton, New Town, Bruntsfield and The Meadows for more coffee adventures.

Madrid

COFFEE FOR THINKERS

Spain's capital is one of those good-living, art-fuelled
cities that makes your gallery-loving heart sing. While
most tourists head to Barcelona, Madrid hums along
with captivating street art, a sensational dining scene,
historic parks, amazing museums like the Prado and
charismatic architecture that spans centuries.

·

You can get a taste of the city's past at the historically and
culturally significant Café Gijón, which was established in
1888 and became a renowned magnet for writers, artists and
left-wing thinkers who would come for coffee and philosophical
or political discussion during the Franco regime. Slip into the
woodsy interior with your travel journal and a cafe con leche
(coffee with hot milk) and feel the history.

Madrid's coffee is still predominantly old school and family run,
where you order your cafe con leche, they pour you a shot and
ask 'calor o frío' (hot or cold milk), but that is changing. The
third-wave is starting to lap on the shores of hip barrios like
Malasaña and Chueca, or you can find good quality coffee at
hole-in-the-wall cafes in the old barrio of Lavapiés. Look out

> **Madrid's coffee is still predominantly old school and family run.**

for cafes and roasters like Hola (its co-founder was the 2016 Barista Champion of Spain and it offers training courses), Toma, Ruda and Federal.

Or you can bridge the historic divide between the old and new at La Libre, a cute, cluttered and quirky cafe-bookshop. There's no wi-fi so forget the laptop and come and soak up the atmosphere and sit with your thoughts – or a good book, instead.

Paris

CAFÉ SOCIÉTÉ

Paris is a sexy beast. Otherworldly patisseries.
Rustic markets. Pungent cheese shops. Sidewalk
cafes. Relaxed, implied style floats through the air
like a subtle perfume.

.

Beyond the Eiffel Tower and the Arc de Triomphe, beyond
the Seine and the wondrous museums and galleries, you'll
find scenic boulevards, curved streets and characterful
arrondissements, full of bistros, boutiques and wrought-
iron balconies.

When it comes to actually thinking about Parisian coffee,
however, your mind will inevitably pirouette to sitting at
a sidewalk cafe – those iconic wicker chairs facing the
street, you sipping coffee, inscrutable behind oversized
sunglasses. You think more of the experience rather than
the coffee itself, which has, up until the last decade or so,
been the understudy rather than the lead. Not anymore.
Now you can get the whole package – with pastry. Great
coffee and French pastry – life rarely gets better.

Your first stop should be the lavish, legendary La Closerie des Lilas in St Germain with its gold-lit interior and rich literary history, where Ernest Hemingway and Henry Miller hung out. Then it's on to the Marais, where you'll find third-wave coffee served in impossibly cinematic cafes like the tiny, blue-painted, six-seater Boot Café, in cosy, brunchy Ob-La-Di, or in La Caféothèque, a temple to specialty coffee.

In the boho 10th arrondissement, around Canal St-Martin, you'll find excellent coffee at La Fontaine de Belleville and specialty brews at Blackburn Coffee.

Keep in mind that it's more expensive to sit down at a cafe than to stand at the bar and have your coffee in Paris. Want it to go? Ask for it 'à emporter'.

Amsterdam

MORE THAN *THOSE* COFFEE SHOPS

With its lacework of canals lined with
17th-century canal houses, Amsterdam is as
pretty as a postcard on the surface and culturally
bountiful underneath, with venerable galleries
like the Rijksmuseum full of Rembrandts and the
Van Gogh Museum.

.

This progressive city is a knock-out on two wheels so make
like a local and take a lazy cycle along the canals and into the
backstreets to unearth a happening vintage boutique, your new
favourite bar or a pocket-sized creative agency brewing up
ideas, or follow your nose to a micro-roaster scenting the lanes.

The Dutch have a long history with coffee, dating back to the
1600s, and a prodigious addiction to it now, with an excellent
local roasting scene and the annual Amsterdam Coffee Festival
in February. And sure, when you think of Amsterdam and
coffee houses, your mind wanders more towards the legalised
greenery (you can actually get a good cup of coffee in some
of those cafes these days), but Amsterdam's coffee scene has
some championship baristas and roasters bringing sustainable
brews to the city. You might also come across the term 'brown

The Dutch have a long history with coffee, dating back to the 1600s, and a prodigious addiction to it now.

cafe' – this just refers to cosy old pubs with brown wooden interiors. They are the complete opposite of Amsterdam's contemporary cafe aesthetic, which is light, bright and airy.

Look out for local roasters and cafes like Bocca (which also runs tastings and barista training) and Espressofabriek, which was one of Amsterdam's earliest specialty coffee roasters. White Label Coffee specialises in single-origin coffees. Other names of sustainable, high-quality note are Screaming Beans, Friedhats (co-founder Lex Wenneker was runner-up in the 2018 World Barista Championships) and micro-roastery Lot Sixty One, which is run by two Australians. For a showcase of Scandinavian beans and their pairings with food, head to Scandinavian Embassy.

Berlin

BARNSTORMING BREWS

Berlin is edgy, creative, sophisticated, indulgent — full of unforgettable street art and history and effervescent with contemporary culture. From riverside beer gardens to punk rock pizza joints, Berlin has a Promethean spirit and energy all its own.

.

If you're on a coffee expedition, make sure you have a traditional 4pm kaffee und kuchen (coffee and cake) at least once. Café Einstein Stammhaus will transport you to elegant times gone by with its natty waiters and starched tablecloths. Or if you want to go super luxe, head to the fabled Hotel Adlon, near the Brandenburg Gate, for afternoon tea in the glamorous lobby.

For less obvious caffeinated destinations, you'll find cafes in old warehouses and garages, in bars closed during the day, and in bright yellow, sci-fi 1960s kiosks (check out Kioski in Kreuzberg). You'll find cafes hidden in secret courtyards and cafes staffed entirely by refugees. And, of course, you'll find super designer coffee houses epitomising Berlin cool. Float around areas like Kreuzkölln, Neukölln, multicultural Kreuzberg and its cafes along the Landwehrkanal, and pretty, tree-lined Oderberger Str in Prenzlauer Berg.

Berlin's specialty roasting scene is relatively young but it is absolutely mighty. If you're a coffee obsessive, roaster The Barn has a worldwide reputation as a fierce champion of ethical and sustainable coffee production, and you might see its beans guest featured in cafes. Its filter coffee is sold black only (espressos can be served with milk), roasted light and clean to showcase the farm-to-cup flavour.

Other excellent cafe–roasteries include Bonanza Coffee, Five Elephant, 19grams and Fjord Coffee Roasters. In the warmer months, try Happy Baristas' nitro on tap, as well as its cheeky coffee-based breakfast cocktails.

HIPSTERS AND HISTORY
Take a daytrip to Leipzig for a great hipster scene. It's also the site of Zum Arabischen Coffe Baum – Germany's oldest coffee house.

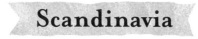

Scandinavia

You could devote an entire tome just to Scandinavian
cafe culture. That world-famous design aesthetic,
countries that rank high on the happiness index,
and eco-friendly cities surrounded by natural
beauty. Oslo and Copenhagen offer all this
and innovative coffee to savour.

•

Norway consumes a staggering amount of coffee and Oslo
has become a hotspot for coffee lovers. It's an innovative and
energetic city, full of parks, ingenious architecture and knock-
out restaurants that hero sustainable produce, and surrounded
by mountains, waterways and forests.

Coffee and Oslo mean two words: Tim Wendelboe. He is a
World Barista Champion and World Cup Tasting Champion and
his eponymous cafe is a pared-back, bare-brick coffee roastery,
espresso bar and coffee school. If you're a coffee obsessive,
Tim Wendelboe is your Stones or Beatles. Oslo likes its coffee
roasted on the lighter side, and paired with Norwegian water
it's an almost scientifically impeccable brew. Look out for
innovative roasters run by award-winners, including Kaffa and
Supreme Roastworks. Damn it, even Oslo's coffee chains like

> •
> You'll be happily
> drinking coffee
> 'til the midnight
> sun sets.
> •

Stockfleths and Norð are great. You'll be happily drinking coffee 'til the midnight sun sets.

Copenhagen is famed for its harbourfront, Nyhavn's colourful houses, 16 Michelin-starred restaurants (yes, including Noma), and contemporary architecture, like the Black Diamond library. In Copenhagen's cafes, you can choose cool simplicity or rock that hygge (a sense of cuddly warmth and conviviality).

Head to the Coffee Collective for a micro-roastery, coffee school and several cafe locations, some with cold coffees (and coffee beers!) on tap. Other excellent places are The Corner at 108, and Prolog, Lagkagehuset and Kaffedepartementet. Have your coffee and a handsomely laden smørrebrød (open sandwich), and take in this picturesque and creative city.

Italy

COFFEE GROUNDS ZERO

Italy — that espresso-fuelled wonderland that has been responsible for igniting so many other coffee cultures across the world. From Melbourne to London to oh-so-many places in between, the wave of mid 20th-century Italian immigration set in motion a wonderful world of coffee drinking and fabulous espresso bars.

.

Most people's first 'proper' cup of coffee was probably at their local Italian coffee bar. That dark espresso and those waistcoated waiters burn deep into the psyche and an unshakeable love of coffee and cafe culture takes hold.

Italy is where brands like Lavazza, Illy, Bialetti moka pots and Gaggia coffee machines come from. It's the language we all speak unwittingly – cappuccino, macchiato, espresso. It's where you'll find ornate, historic cafes with suave waiters in white with black bowties. It's where impossibly charismatic people have a quick shot of espresso at the bar. And it's where you'll actually find The University of Coffee (run by Illy in Trieste).

Coffee and cafes are everywhere, but Italy's longest-running cafes are things of unimaginable beauty and their atmosphere is almost edible. Roscioli Caffè in Rome is one of those outrageously luscious patisseries, delis and wine stores that is a gastronomic overload. Visit Gran Caffè Gambrinus in Naples to pick up a cuccuma (a traditional Neapolitan coffee pot) and linger over coffee in the same place that Oscar Wilde and Ernest Hemingway once did. Antico Caffè Torinese in Trieste is an Art Nouveau beauty with its curves and sleek wooden bar and fulsome chandelier. Venice's Caffè Florian (established in 1720, making it Italy's oldest continuous cafe) is a lavish celebration of gilt mirrors, velvet seating and elaborately painted ceilings. Is it any wonder both Lord Byron and Casanova were apparently regulars? These few are mere grains of sugar in the vast cup of Italy's swoon-worthy coffee institutions.

If you're travelling throughout Italy, just as regions have their specialty produce or signature dishes, so will they have their own spin on coffee – try a creamy, chocolatey bicerin in Turin (*see* recipe p. 22), or caffè alla valdostana (coffee with lemon peel, cinnamon, sugar, cloves, sometimes alcohol) shared from a friendship cup in the Aosta Valley in northern Italy. In Padua, patavina is espresso, cream and a little mint syrup, and Calabrian coffee contains a hit of licorice. Too warm for espresso? Order a shakerato (espresso and simple syrup shaken over ice and strained into a martini glass) or do like some Sicilians do in summer and swap out a morning cappuccino for a coffee granita with whipped cream. Speaking of morning cappuccinos, that's exactly where they stay in Italy. Italians only have milk-based coffee drinks before 11am.

If you love cafe culture, you'll be a kid in a candy store no matter where you go in Italy, but for a truly cinematic twist, check out Bar Luce in Milan – designed by film director Wes Anderson.

However, as deeply traditional as Italy's coffee scene is, there is some third-wave action happening, with specialty roasters crafting an interesting strand in the next iteration of this iconic coffee culture.

MONK-Y BUSINESS

Fun story – cappuccino gets its name from the Capuchin friars, an order of Franciscan monks founded in Italy in the 16th century, because their hooded robes were almost the same colour as espresso mixed with milk.

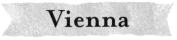

Vienna

SACHER IT TO ME

Settle into a red velvet armchair bathed in the
golden glow of twinkling chandeliers. Take your
time perusing the papers, with your coffee and one
slender, gleaming, perfect slice of Vienna's famed
chocolate and apricot sacher torte by your side.

.

Vienna's opulent coffee palaces are the rightful and wondrous
stuff of legend. Sit under the grand, vaulting arches of the
historic Café Central or sink into the slightly more restrained
Café Landtmann.

For all its gilt and fine china, Vienna's actually got quite a sassy
coffee history dating back to the 17th century and involving
sacks of coffee beans being dumped by fleeing Turks at the
end of the Siege of Vienna, a local snapping the beans up and
getting the first licence to sell coffee, and Vienna's first coffee
house being opened by an Armenian spy in 1720.

It was that coffee house (Kramersches Kaffeehaus) that melded
the art of coffee and conversation by putting out newspapers
for people to read, creating an opulent honeypot for the city's
intellectuals to gather.

> Vienna's opulent coffee palaces are the rightful and wondrous stuff of legend.

Vienna's coffee house culture has been a rollercoaster due to wars, economic crises and fading fashions – the Italian-style espresso bars of the 1950s made the grand old coffee houses seem rather passé. But in 1983, 300 years after that initial coffee discovery, a new appreciation of Vienna's unique coffee houses fired up a revival and, in 2011, Viennese coffee house culture was added to UNESCO's Intangible Cultural Heritage List.

For a more contemporary experience, Gota Coffee is a cafe–roastery that offers seasonal blends and coffee workshops. CaffèCouture champions a light roast to highlight the bean flavours. Decor might be the antithesis of the grand old palaces, but it's the coffee that's the star attraction. Go wandering areas like Neubau for a taste of Vienna right now.

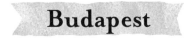

Budapest

THE TASTIEST TIME TRAVEL

Park the present while you're in Budapest, and go old-school glamorous. Sure, there's no shortage of third-wave coffee, but it's the cafes of the past that will blow you away.

·

Budapest is a stunner. Bisected by the Danube, it's a glorious melange of Baroque and Art Nouveau architecture, street food and street art. It's a treasure trove of hidden courtyards and handsome hot springs. But as a coffee lover, you can do some serious time travel here.

Trip back to the turn of the 20th century, when Budapest's coffee culture gave rise to hundreds of glamorous cafes across the city, turning them into lavish meeting places for writers, poets and artists. For some perfect examples, visit Café Gerbeaud, opened in 1858 and one of Europe's oldest cafes, or Café Central. Make a reservation at the fabulous-looking New York Café in the New York Palace Hotel, which was restored to its Italian Renaissance grandeur in 2006 and is a wonderland of gilt and sparkling chandeliers.

Travelling further forward in time, the communist regime spelled the end of many luxurious cafes, and gave rise to a more austere version, known as an eszpresszó. There are still a few of these about – try Bambi or Táskarádió Coffee for a retro experience.

Which brings us to now, where you'll find incredibly hip cafes like The Goat Herder in all corners of the city. Head to the Jewish Quarter for a concentrated bite of Budapest's contemporary cafe and culture scene.

CAKES FIT FOR A QUEEN
Do visit Ruszwurm, Budapest's oldest coffee house. It opened in 1827 and its cakes were (and are) so delicious that Elisabeth, Empress of Austria and Queen of Hungary (1837–98), would send someone out to fetch them for her breakfast. Respect.

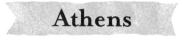

Athens

It might feel surreal to order a pour-over in view
of the Acropolis, while sitting in the seat of the
great philosophers, but being a creative city it's
hardly surprising that third-wave coffee is being
embraced in Athens.

·

Coffee has always been part of the fabric of life in Athens.
A traditional Greek coffee is made by putting water, sugar and
fine Greek coffee in a briki (a small, jug-like saucepan) and
bringing it to the boil until there's a layer of kaimaki (foam) on
top. You then take it off the heat to settle, spoon some foam
in each cup, then add the brewed coffee. You can get it all
over the city but it's particularly tasty if you head out into the
mountain villages and have it made by a yiayia (grandmother).
You might find it useful to know that sketos is without sugar,
metrios is one teaspoon of sugar, and glykos means sweet.

Yiannis Taloumis's Taf Coffee was one of the first specialty coffee cafes in Athens. It has an onsite roastery and some awarded baristas, but still offers a traditional Greek coffee. LOT51 is another roaster pushing Athens's specialty coffee scene, as is Nomad. The Underdog is a clean, pared-back cafe–roastery in a Neoclassical building, owned by an award-winning barista. Its resident roaster brought home the Greek championship in 2018 so you're guaranteed an unforgettable cup here.

KEEP IT COOL

Iced coffee has been popular since the '50s and it's drunk all year round in Greece. Frappé is a foamy concoction made by shaking up instant coffee, water, ice cubes and sugar (*see* p. 22). Freddo Espresso is espresso blitzed with ice and sugar to make a foamy, cold espresso, and Freddo Cappuccino is a chilled version of a cappuccino.

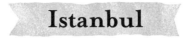

Istanbul

LOVE IN A CUP

There's an old Turkish proverb: 'Coffee should
be black as hell, strong as death, and sweet as love'.
Turkish coffee is rich in history, hospitality and
custom, from reading coffee grounds to testing
potential suitors and for family celebrations.
It's such a rich tradition that it's on UNESCO's
Intangible Cultural Heritage List.

.

With its feet in two continental camps, Istanbul is a vast and
diverse city with a historic centre that's a marvel of mosques
and minarets, water views, Ottoman-era architecture and
captivating bazaars.

You can peek into the coffee trade of the Ottoman past by
wandering Istanbul's wondrous, epic Grand Bazaar. Or you
can explore the historic Kadıköy Bazaar, and have a traditional
Turkish coffee experience at Fazıl Bey, sipping coffee and
soaking up the market vibes. Coffee here is intrinsically woven
into the fabric of everyday social life. It's as much about the
brew as it is about your crew.

> Coffee here is intrinsically woven into the fabric of everyday social life.

Turkish coffee is deliciously potent. Using an ibrik or cezve (a small, tapered pot with a long handle), water is added, plus sugar to taste, and brought to a boil. Very, very finely ground coffee is then added and returned to the heat to come to the boil two more times. Once the coffee has settled, it's gently poured into small coffee cups and served with something fragrant and sweet, like Turkish delight or baklava (*see* recipe p. 20).

Istanbul is also embracing the third-wave. Areas like Moda in Kadıköy have an artsy vibe and a high concentration of contemporary cafes. Look out for roasters like Montag who offer a wide range of single-origins, or Coffeetopia's Cup of Excellence beans. For the best of the old and the new, seek out Story Coffee, located within an Ottoman-era building.

Africa &
the Middle East

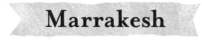

Marrakesh

MAGICAL MYSTERY BREWS

Morocco's mesmerising Red City is a sensory
whirlwind of mosques and ancient history, secret
gardens, ornately tiled architecture, calls to prayer
and a tangle of beguiling laneways where artisans
work their craft.

·

Dive into Marrakesh's bustling, historical medina and its
swarming souqs (marketplaces), or get into the spirit of the
golden-lit outdoor party in Jemaa el-Fnaa, the sprawling central
square that erupts into a fiesta of roving performers, snake
charmers, jubilant music and sizzling street food every night.

While mint tea is the beverage most often associated with
Marrakesh, there's a definite coffee culture. Here, espresso
is to be savoured. It's something to take your time over. To
have meetings over. Something to conduct all the business
of life over.

If you happen upon a coffee vendor in a souq, you can buy
freshly ground spiced coffee – select the spices you want, say
cloves, cinnamon, nutmeg or black pepper, and they'll grind the
spices in with your beans. If you're ordering coffee in a cafe,
your two basic options are cafe noir or nous nous. Cafe noir

is essentially a small cup of espresso. Nous nous translates to half and half. It's half milk and half espresso – steam the milk first, then let the espresso drip down into it.

For a third-wave coffee hit, seek out the American-run Bloom Coffee, where you can grab an excellent single-origin or get some specialty beans and coffee equipment to take back to your riad (courtyard house converted into a boutique hotel).

If you want your coffee with a side of unbelievably stylish Marrakesh glamour, head to the Bacha Coffeehouse in the Musée des Confluences (Dar el Bacha), with its velvet and rattan furnishings, arching plants, gleaming checkerboard tiles and an encyclopaedia of top-notch single-origin beans. Or have coffee on the rooftop terrace at the hyper-chic Nomad, taking in the views of the Red City and beyond to the Atlas Mountains.

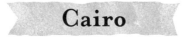

Cairo

The thought of the River Nile or those mystical pyramids might seem slow and soothing, but Cairo, pulsating on the banks of the famed river, is quite the opposite — a high-octane, sprawling metropolis where calls to prayer weave around the urban melee. It's a clash of thrilling antiquities, bustling bazaars, shisha lounges and sizzling, aromatic street food.

•

Egypt was one of coffee's first stops on its journey into the wider world, landing in Cairo from the Yemeni port of Mocha in the 16th century. By the end of the 17th century, there were hundreds of ahwas (coffee houses) in Cairo, becoming lively hubs for political and literary conversation.

The classic ahwa experience means a leisurely time spent with coffee (or tea), a shisha and a board game, like chess. Coffee here is traditionally similar to Turkish coffee – powder-fine coffee grounds are added to a kanaka (small pot) with water and brought to a foamy heat, then poured into small cups. Because it's made with sweetened water (unsweetened coffee is for sad occasions, like funerals), you can order it arriha (sweet), mazboot (medium sweet) or ziyada (*really* sweet).

> The classic ahwa experience means a leisurely time spent with coffee (or tea), a shisha and a board game, like chess.

You can add aromatic spices, and it's perfect with a piece of syrupy almond and semolina cake.

Seek out El Fishawy, near the Khan el-Khalili souq – it's been operating since 1797! Or follow the scent of roasting beans to Al-Ghoreya, a cosy, old-time, ornamented cafe–roastery that started selling beans in 1830. Shaheen is a third-generation family business that has been roasting since 1937. And then there's Café Riche, established in 1908, a timewarp cafe famous for hosting literary and political heavyweights.

For Cairo's contemporary coffee scene, Café Greco and Coffee Corner are reliable stalwarts, or head to Espresso Lab for a cold brew.

Tel Aviv

BEACHSIDE CAPITAL OF COOL

A culturally diverse, artistically engaged city set against a backdrop of the shimmering Mediterranean Sea, Tel Aviv is a high-energy maelstrom of style and wonder. It's an utterly unique blend of beaches, Bauhaus architecture, thriving high-tech, major museums, galleries and opera houses, with a showstopping restaurant scene and a high concentration of great vegan eateries.

•

Unsurprisingly, Tel Aviv has some super-stylish cafes, often with great outdoor spaces. You'll find excellent coffee all across the city, so it's a good excuse to explore the arched, cobbled laneways of Old Jaffa, or White City, the central part of town that is UNESCO-listed for its incredible Bauhaus architecture. You also shouldn't miss the labyrinth of the Jaffa Flea Market, the artsy, boho area of Florentin or the tranquil, sophisticated Neve Tzedek.

The coffee palate in Tel Aviv tends towards darker roasts but there is no end of third-wave roasters offering their take on coffee. Aroma is the main home-grown chain (for a caffeine-free alternative, try its hot soy with halva) but there are some top-notch micro-roasters roasting sustainable beans and crafting V60 filters to showcase their flavours.

Look out for roasters like Cafelix or grab some beans from Nahat, a cafe–roastery that promotes a farm-to-cup ethos and can brew you up an espresso, a French press or a Clever Coffee Dripper. Sit on the vine-twined terrace of Coffee Shop 51 and savour its seasonal microlots, particularly good as a filter, which the baristas here are especially focused on.

Spacious and minimal WayCup Coffee (get it? Wake up?) roasts up some especially good beans for espresso. Micro-roaster Edmund goes dark and fruity on its roasts, but also batches up a cold brew to go. Its lush hidden courtyard cafe accessed through an inconspicuous walkway is the ultimate in restrained Tel Aviv style.

Oh, and a quick language lesson: 'café shachor' is Hebrew for black coffee, and if you see 'café hafuch' on a menu, it's an upside-down cafe latte, where milk goes in first, then espresso, then foam.

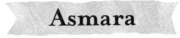

Asmara

AFRICAN DECO DELIGHT

Africa — specifically Ethiopia — is the real, actual birthplace of coffee. Still one of the world's biggest coffee producers, Africa is a coffee lover's dream odyssey — you can visit plantations and museums and take part in coffee ceremonies. A surprising destination that teams Art Deco with Italian coffee culture and the African experience is Asmara in Eritrea.

.

When the sun goes down, the locals come out to stroll and socialise and take in the evening from an outdoor cafe, against a backdrop of colourful Deco buildings.

Once called Little Rome, Asmara was under Italian rule from 1890 to 1941 and was transformed into an Italianate and Art Deco city with wide boulevards and a decidedly Italian coffee culture, which pairs nicely with the traditional coffee drinking ceremonies of Eritrea. Make sure you dip in to both styles – stop in for a classic espresso at an Italian cafe, then settle in for a more leisurely traditional ceremony, where you drink a round of three miniature cups of coffee from the same pot.

THE TRADITIONAL
ETHIOPIAN COFFEE CEREMONY

Fresh grass cuttings are scattered and fragrant incense burns while your host roasts green coffee beans on the stove, releasing a spectacular coffee aroma that blends with the incense. The host then grinds the roasted beans in a mortar and pestle, brews it and pours it from a jebena (clay jug) into tiny cups with lots of sugar. You have three rounds of this from the same jug – the very last round is considered a blessing. And it is, to be part of such a poetic ceremony in the birthplace of the bean.

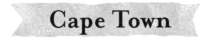

Cape Town

COFFEE TABLE MOUNTAIN

When a city has a stunning natural backdrop called
Table Mountain, it's hardly surprising that Cape
Town is a culinary wonderland. It's a creative,
multicultural and design-centric city, home to
jaw-dropping wineries, a vibrant food scene —
and great coffee.

·

Although Cape Town's contemporary coffee scene is a
relatively young one, it has bloomed with caffeinated gusto.
Instant coffee (including Ricoffy, a blend of coffee and chicory)
was the name of the game until the second-wave hit, and
local chains like Seattle Coffee Company kicked off in the
late '90s. With the turn of the millennium, the coffee scene
shifted into high gear, creating a vibrant coffee culture of
micro-roasteries, inventive cafes, barista training opportunities
and coffee-related events.

With the turn of the millennium, the coffee scene shifted into high gear.

Coffee menus are up there with the best of them, offering V60s, nitro cold brews, you name it. Explore hip areas like Woodstock, or head to the candy-coloured streets like De Waterkant for chic boutiques, bars and cafes, and Bo-Kaap for Cape Malay cuisine and corner cafes. Look out for cafe–roasteries like Origin, Rosetta, Bean There, Espresso Lab, Deluxe Coffeeworks and Tribe.

Cape Town is also home to the much-lauded, highly stylised, steampunk-themed Truth Coffee Roasting, where exposed pipes, hissing coffee machines and staff in scuffed-up, steampunk couture serve you your single-origin. (It has been voted the world's best coffee house by more than one source. Truth.)

Asia

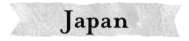

Japan

LO-FI TO SCI-FI

From up-to-the-minute or way back in time, from coffee in a can to handcrafted pour-overs, Japan's coffee culture is as wondrous as its homeland.

.

Tokyo is magical. The crowds negotiating the hashtag of crossings at neon-drenched Shibuya. The narrow, haphazard streets of Shimokitazawa with its canopy of powerlines and ramshackle vintage stores. The jewellery-box department stores of Ginza and the record stores and rowdy izakayas (bars) of Koenji. And the coffee.

For coffee lovers, seeing that first vending machine stacked with canned coffee on the street is when you *know* Tokyo is your happy place. Coffee's everywhere here – at the 7-Eleven, in litre-cartons at the supermarket and in chains serving cherry blossom frappuccino.

For specialty coffee, Tokyo's baristas are part artist, part scientist, so dip into the minimalist Koffee Mameya, Single O in Sumida or the sci-fi Roastery by Nozy. For eccentric, old-school kicks, don't miss the knick-knacky, retro kissatens (coffee houses).

Osaka has a gorgeous, knockabout vibe to it. Pulsing neon bounces off the canals in Dotonbori. Old-fashioned shotengai (local shopping streets and covered arcades) offer everything from watch repairs to Osaka's famous street snack, takoyaki (octopus balls). Narrow laneways are peppered with tiny thrills – record bars, miniature bakeries and nutty details in every window.

Also known as 'the kitchen of Japan', Osaka has the motto kuidaore (eat until you drop). For a city so food-focused, it's no surprise that Osaka knows its way around an excellent coffee experience, too.

You'll find totally groovy old-school kissatens like Junkissa American or Mazura – eccentric explosions of mid-century decor, serving coffee and dainty sandwiches with a smoky, jazzy backdrop. Osaka is also home to both global and local chains, and pared-back, hyper-stylish cafes like Takamura Wine and Coffee Roasters. Wander the tiny streets of Nakazakicho for whimsical coffee houses like Café Taiyou No Tou and Melbourne-style cafe Pathfinder XNOBU.

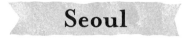

Seoul

CITY OF CAFE STREETS

A dynamic metropolis surrounded by mountains,
Seoul is a high-speed glamour clash of old and new,
where tech meets temples and food and fashion
are serious business. As serious as the business of
drinking coffee.

·

Despite being the city with the most Starbucks in the world,
the home-grown specialty coffee scene here is a creative and
diverse one, with a unique take on the cafe experience. (It's
also the location of the 2007 TV series *Coffee Prince*, which
was set in a cafe and managed to meld specialty coffee with
gripping romance!)

The beauty of drinking coffee in Seoul is the environment.
You can find yourself sipping a cafe latte and taking in the
scenery at one of the many coffee houses on the bridges of
the Han River or in a hanok (a converted traditional house).
You can find yourself soaking up the smell of beans roasting
within the industrial chic of a converted factory.

> The home-grown specialty coffee scene here is a creative and diverse one, with a unique take on the cafe experience.

Seoul cafes can be as architecturally addictive as the coffee. Manufact Coffee Roasters is the perfect exercise in hypnotic minimalism.

Seoul also has 'cafe streets' (could there be any better place for a coffee-loving traveller?), which are exactly what they sound like. Streets like Yeonnam-dong are lined with idiosyncratic coffee houses, many in revamped private homes. You'll find cafes themed around flowers, or particular cities or countries, or you'll find Parisian-style 'book cafes' that attract coffee lovers for some intellectual debate.

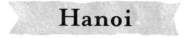

Hanoi

COOL AND SWEET

Vietnam's capital buzzes from dawn to dusk and beyond, but there's light and shade in the experience. Hanoi is a mix of graceful architecture, artisan shops and lakes with bobbing pedal boats alongside the clatter and steam of street food and seas of motorbikes whizzing in all directions.

.

So your first coffee in Hanoi has to be a classic cà phê sữa đá (iced coffee). Your cup will come with a small metal cup and filter perched on top, and deep, dark coffee will slowly drip through the filter into your cup. You'll add condensed milk and a handful of ice cubes and stir them through for a strong, sweet, cooling caffeine hit (*see* recipe p. 21).

Then, of course, you're going to have to try the other famous brew – cà phê trứng (egg coffee). Stay with me. A whipped combination of egg yolk, condensed milk, butter and cheese is added to strong filter coffee and served sitting in a bowl of hot water to keep it drinkably warm. It's been described as 'liquid tiramisu' and has a rich dessert vibe.

You'll find third-wave glamour spots in Hanoi too – places like the quirky, cosy Kafeville, with its dark wood tables and pretty windows onto the street.

The best Hanoi coffee moment is had by slipping down a narrow alleyway, up some rickety stairs to a second-floor outdoor patio of a fading French colonial-era building where, under twinkling fairy lights and a lazily spinning fan, you can take your time as you stir the ice in your coffee and take in the blur of the bikes and busyness below.

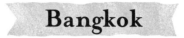

Bangkok

Bangkok is a cosmopolitan hive of street food and neon, glamour malls and buzzing traffic, ancient temples and lazy rivers. A fascinating blend of lo-fi tradition and high-tech style, the city is one sprawling, delicious dynamo.

·

Thailand's coffee production only kicked off in earnest in the 1970s, but Bangkok has leapt onto the third-wave of coffee – and with incredible style. Most specialty coffee is grown in northern, mountainous Thailand and delivers a clean, sweet, slightly spicy flavour, while the south only grows robusta.

Many cafes showcase Thailand's coffee, like the sleek Ceresia Coffee Roasters in Klongton Nua that uses seasonal beans from single-origin farms. Then there's Roots (multiple locations), an industrial-chic cafe–roastery that promotes the beans of Northern Thailand (and makes a super refreshing espresso tonic, mixing cold brew with orange syrup and topping it off with tonic water and ice).

Look out for photogenic places like the minimalist Hands and Heart (Brewers Cup champions), which hand-grinds beans for your drip or AeroPress. Head to the quaint, indie area of Phra Khanong Nuea to check out the single-origin pour-overs (and the art-filled, bare-brick walls) at Ink and Lion, as well as the exceptional espresso (and coffee-based cocktails) at the plant-covered Sometimes I Feel.

Bangkok is hot and humid – that's why there's some top-notch cold brews. Rocket Coffeebar in Silom makes its cold brew by infusing chilled mineral water with its espresso blend for 24 hours and then filtering it. Brave Roasters makes a French press, infuses it with citrus or spices and then chills it.

Dive into busy, cafe-filled areas like Sukhumvit or check out newer community initiatives like theCOMMONS – two contemporary mini-malls (in Thonglor and Saladaeng) that include markets, outdoor play spaces, artisan producers and happening cafes and eateries.

•

Bangkok has leapt onto the third-wave of coffee — and with incredible style.

•

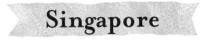

Singapore

COFFEE IN A GARDEN

Known as the 'City in a Garden', Singapore has shimmering silver skyscrapers that spill luscious foliage from their densely forested terraces, while Gardens by the Bay, Fort Canning Park and Singapore Botanic Gardens bring lavish chunks of nature. Singapore is a super-stylish, food-obsessed melting pot, and there's a passionate professional coffee culture too. Coffee here swings from traditional to third-wave, and is often a blend of the two.

·

The traditional coffee is kopi (black coffee with condensed milk). Robusta beans are wok-roasted with sugar and margarine, then ground. The coffee is put into a long fabric sock, then boiling water is poured over from a tall, thin silver kettle. Head to one of the bustling, sizzling hawker markets for a serve, perhaps with some kaya toast.

For a blend of the old and the new, go to family-run Coffee Break in the Amoy Street hawker centre. The third-generation of this simple stall serves up old-school brew methods and new-school twists, like a black sesame cafe latte.

For a dose of third-wave coffee, you'll find design-driven cafe–roasteries, some with labs and academies for cupping sessions and latte art classes. Explore areas like eclectic Haji Lane and Arab Street with its colourful shophouses, or neighbourhoods like Tiong Bahru, a creative enclave of cafes and boutiques; and look out for roasters like Nylon, Common Man, Papa Palheta and Dutch Colony, among others.

LUXE IT UP
If you really want to push the boat out, why not treat yourself to coffee and afternoon tea at one of Singapore's swanky hotels? There's a number of luxury options, including the Fullerton and the Marina Bay Sands, or you could opt for the iconic Raffles Hotel – it has its own custom coffee blend. Buy some beans to take home!

Bali

RIDING THE COFFEE WAVES

When you think of Bali, beautiful beaches and chill-
out resorts might spring to mind. But while you're
ordering your poolside cocktail, you might not realise
that you're also lounging within one of the world's
biggest coffee producers.

·

Bali has huge plantations in the island's central and northern
highlands, particularly in Kintamani. While Bali grows arabica
beans, the bulk of Balinese-grown coffee is robusta, tending
towards a full-bodied, smoky flavour with low acidity. You
can tour many of the plantations – Batukaru Coffee Estate
and Retreat, halfway up the slopes of Mount Batukaru, is a
fascinating biodynamic coffee plantation that also offers lush
accommodation, yoga and farm-to-table dining.

Bali is famous for its street food so start off with a traditional
kopi tubruk (thick, black coffee with sugar, and you leave the
'mud' behind when you drink it) from a warung (local street
stand). It's not dissimilar to Turkish coffee. Once you've ticked
that off, you can dip into areas like Canggu (try the coffee at
Crate and Machinery Cafe) and Uluwatu (try Drifter or Suka
Espresso) and happen upon stylish, breezy cafes that are

brewing up beautiful third-wave coffee (including excellent cold brews to beat the heat), making the most of the beans grown on their doorstep.

Ubud is Bali's cultural capital, big on wellness, home to yoga retreats, writers' festivals, culinary delights and, yes, amazing coffee. You'll find gorgeous cafes tucked into the hills and side streets, but if you want to get deep into Balinese coffee, head to Seniman Coffee for a hand-brewed coffee, a bag of freshly roasted beans and a roasting demonstration or up your coffee skills with one of its many workshops.

PARTY POOPER

Kopi luwak, 'the world's most expensive coffee', is harvested from the faeces of wild civet cats. (Eeuw.) If you care about animals, give it a miss as most of these tourist-trapping beans are the result of highly unethical practices.

Australia &
New Zealand

AUSTRALIA

NEW ZEALAND

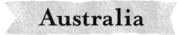

Australia

A BIG BEAN SCENE

You can surf all the coffee waves here, from brews with glamorous views to countercultural cafes within one of the world's biggest coffee destinations. You'll find great coffee all over Australia, but Melbourne, Sydney and Byron Bay will have coffee-lovers swooning.

.

If Melbourne were a perfume, it would be a blend of black coffee and tangy egg-poaching water on a crisp winter breeze. Famed for its street-art laneways, this UNESCO City of Literature is fuelled by a steady diet of indie bookstores and boutiques, innovative eateries and renegade theatre.

Melbourne's coffee scene started in the coffee palaces of the temperance movement in the 1880s. By the 1950s, Italian immigrants had founded iconic cafes like Pellegrini's and created a Little Italy in Carlton and, by the 1980s, Marios in Fitzroy started doing all-day breakfasts for its late-sleeping, bohemian clientele, kick-starting the brunch and cafe culture the city thrives on today. Since then, Melbourne has brewed up a trail-blazing, award-winning coffee scene. Specialty coffee made by expert baristas is available all across the city, the knowledge of the average coffee drinker is high, and many toddlers' first word is 'babycino'!

Looks-wise, Melbourne cafes, many with onsite roasters, tend to the quasi-industrial (St Ali, Axil) and Scandi-centric (Dukes), but you'll also find rustic Italian cafes playing '60s soul music, corner stores converted to cosy coffee pads, and minimal, sci-fi brew bars like Sensory Lab.

There's no getting around it. Sydney's a stunner. Those broad postcard beaches, the Harbour, the Opera House, the Bridge, hidden coves, that blue sky that seems to have been photoshopped. And while Sydney might be thought of as more of a sun and surf kind of destination, its coffee scene really is no slouch.

Sydney's brunch scene kicked off in the early '90s with the advent of Bills and his famous ricotta hotcakes, but come the turn of the new millennium there were roasters like Campos, Toby's Estate and Reuben Hills switching up the coffee playing field. Current-day Sydney is a thriving hot bed of glamorously cool cafe spaces and top-notch roasters championing ethical, sustainable beans, with a leaning towards a lighter roast.

Head to areas like Newtown and Sydney's inner west for groovy cafes, and gentrified Surry Hills for great coffee at Paramount or Reformatory. And I definitely recommend you saddle up for a coffee flight from the single-origin batch coffee taps at superstar roasters Single O. Yep, you read that right. Coffee on tap. Coffee. On. Tap. Who said dreams can't come true?

Countercultural Byron Bay is an iconic coastal surf town on Australia's east coast. Famed for its wellness retreats and artisanal, organic ethos, its streets are a charming tumble of buskers, backpackers, boutique stores, yoga beauties and celebrities chilling right out.

No surprise, then, that Byron's coffee is completely off the charts. From tiny holes-in-the-wall to airy, green spaces like Folk and Bayleaf and laidback shacks like The Top Shop, an incredible cup of coffee is a given.

If you want to explore Byron coffee from seed to cup, visit Zentveld's coffee plantation and farm-based roastery in nearby Newrybar.

New Zealand

SHORT BLACKS AND LONG WHITE CLOUDS

New Zealand is something of a caffeine powerhouse
with its coffee culture, its championing of ethically
sourced beans and its award-winning baristas.
Whether it's in Auckland or 'Windy Welly'
Wellington, your coffee experience will combine
crisp air and stunning natural beauty with an
invigorated creative spirit, indie sensibility and
a food scene that celebrates its local produce.

.

Wellington's caffeinated history has its roots in the milk bars
of the 1930s and the Eurocentric coffee houses of the 1950s
that attracted a boho clientele. It's the birthplace of famed
Coffee Supreme, started in the early '90s, with outposts
in both Melbourne and Tokyo. Flight Coffee is yet another
Wellington wonder with an owner who placed in the World
Barista Championships.

This city is teeming with micro-roasters who offer brews with
traceability, and innovative cafes with vaulted interiors, lively
menus and local roasts. Look out for Red Rabbit Coffee Co.,
Peoples Coffee, L'affare and Havana Coffee Works, one of
the city's oldest roasters. Head to inner-city Te Aro – a pretty

> *Your coffee experience will combine crisp air and stunning natural beauty.*

waterfront area boasting cafes, cinemas, indie theatres, galleries and restaurants.

Auckland's indie cafe scene has evolved to feature more roasteries, and famed boho cafe DKD is now solely a roastery. The city is the birthplace of Allpress, which started as a coffee cart in the '80s after Michael Allpress got inspired by Seattle's coffee revival, and now supplies its lovely roasts all over the world.

Atomic is another Auckland big-hitter, roasting since the early '90s and offering a tasting tray of the house blend – espresso, cold brew and piccolo. Kokako roasts up top-notch fairtrade beans and sells them in compostable packaging. Head to Ponsonby Road for happening boutiques, bistros and charismatic cafes, but, really, you'll find a superb brew anywhere here.

Acknowledgements

Books and coffee are my two favourite things, so a big, brewed thank you to Hardie Grant, and especially to Melissa Kayser, Megan Cuthbert, Alice Barker, Alexandra Payne, Michelle Mackintosh, Megan Ellis, Rosanna Dutson and Wenjia Tang for bringing these two together.

Thank you to Santana Rudge, Carolyn Bain and Karen Martin for your on-the-ground recommendations.

To all the wonderful coffee professionals – Dion Cohen, Michelle Duong, Shinsaku Fukayama, Andy Gelman, Paul Henry, Kamaka Hoopai, Jonathan Riethmaier and Bec Zentveld – I had a blast talking with you all and I salute your passion.

Thanks and kisses to Mum, Dad, Helen, Martin, Aidan and Max. I love you as much as the brew. To Steve and Michelle for all your advice. To William, Phu, Linda and Sara. To George, Paula, Rose and Bridget (go Iowa!), and Jane and Andy. To the LLPPP. To my Bay Area crew, Janet, Vivek, Ishaan and Arden, and to Chris Baty, who made me drink so much coffee I climbed Indian Rock in Fluevog heels. To Ali, Caz, Lesley, Sam, Lukay, Kara Lynne, Lovey, Danny, Trent, Ty, Enrique, Pete Bovell and Suzy Shaw. To Jasna Fletcher for always putting out a nice tray. And to my sweetheart, Chris Foley, for keeping his Queen of Sheba in coffee and books.

About the author

Jane Ormond has written about food and travel for the last two decades. She has written for Lonely Planet, Jetstar, Icelandair, *The Age Good Food Guide*, *The Age Good Cafe Guide*, *Cheap Eats*, *Gourmet Traveller* and *Good Food*, among others. She lives in Melbourne, one of the world's greatest coffee cities, which is handy for someone with a lifelong obsession with coffee.

About the illustrator

Wenjia Tang is a freelance illustrator who graduated from Maryland Institute College of Art in 2017. She was born in south-east China, and went to the United States for high school when she was 15. She loves all kinds of animals, and lives with a cat in Manhattan, New York.

Her work has been recognised by American Illustration, Society of Illustrators, *Communication Arts*, AOI, *3x3 Magazine* and more.

Published in 2021 by Hardie Grant Travel,
a division of Hardie Grant Publishing

Hardie Grant Travel (Melbourne)
Building 1, 658 Church Street
Richmond, Victoria 3121

Hardie Grant Travel (Sydney)
Level 7, 45 Jones Street
Ultimo, NSW 2007

www.hardiegrant.com/au/travel

A catalogue record for this
book is available from the
National Library of Australia

Hardie Grant acknowledges the Traditional Owners of the country on
which we work, the Wurundjeri people of the Kulin nation and the
Gadigal people of the Eora nation, and recognises their continuing
connection to the land, waters and culture. We pay our respects to
their Elders past, present and emerging.

Destination Coffee
ISBN 9781741176902

10 9 8 7 6 5 4 3 2 1

Publisher	**Editor**	**Design**
Melissa Kayser	Alice Barker	Michelle Mackintosh
Project manager	**Proofreader**	**Typesetting**
Alexandra Payne	Rosanna Dutson	Megan Ellis
Senior editor		
Megan Cuthbert		

Colour reproduction by Megan Ellis and Splitting Image Colour Studio
Printed and bound in China by LEO Paper Products LTD.